Where Flies The Bird?

Written & Designed

by

Latoya Belfon

Creative Consultant Zidina Hoyte

Where flies the bird?

Do you know? I've not heard,

Their songs in the morning's first dew.

There's a cold change in weather,
So they've gathered together,
With many a plan to fly soon.

WHERE FLIES THE BIRD?

DO YOU KNOW? I'VE NOT HEARD!

I'VE ASKED THE FROGS BY THE POND.

They too do not know,

But are packed, ready to go,

But the birds I've not heard, not a sound.

Where flies the bird?

do you know? I've not heard!

Lift-off is happening today!

They've joined up together,
With winged v-shaped feathers,
because snow is almost on its way.

Where flew the bird?
Do you know? I've not heard!
Winter greets us with hello!

THE WINDS, COLD AND BRISK

BRING SNOWFLAKES ON A WISP,

STILL, NO ANSWER TO WHERE'D THE BIRDS GO!

WHERE FLEW THE BIRD?
do you know? I've not heard!
THE SUN HAS RETURNED TO STAY.

Flowers are blooming
Green leafed branches dancing,
Spring has now made its way.

WHERE FLEW THE BIRD?

DO YOU KNOW? YES, I KNOW!

MAMA BIRD FLIES TO MY AIDE.

The whole flock has returned,
no more cause for concern,
I am eager to know where they stayed.

Where flew the bird?
Do you know? "yes, I know!"
"We travelled from north to south."

When cold winds come closer.

We travel together.

For warm sights and more food for our mouths.

Alas! That explains why.
Fewer birds were in the sky
And morning songs I could not hear.

Frogs, too, had no clue.

Badger, yes, him too!

I even asked a lost deer.

HA! NO, YOU SEE,
WHEN WE FEEL THE COLD BREEZE,
WE KNOW THAT SNOWFLAKES ARE NEAR.

So bird's nests are empty
ducks and goose packed and ready,
and butterflies travel with care.

SO WHERE FLIES THE BIRD?
Do you know? Yes, I've heard!
They'll travel to a sunshine state.

They'll fly in a hurry
Together, so don't worry,
They'll be safe from the cold winter's fate.

TRAVEL
SAFE

Happy
MIGRATING!

Are you able to guess what animal

 **is migrating here?**

It swims very far for warmer waters for as long as 28 days.

Educational Fun Fact

Did you know that The bar-tailed godwit can fly for nearly 7,000 miles without stopping, making it the bird with the longest recorded non-stop flight?

That is a very long time to fly without eating!

How many times do you eat a day?

CAN YOU READ THESE MIGRATION WORDS?

NORTH	SOUTH
SWIM	WIN-TER
NEST	AN-I-MALS
WARM	FLY
	MI-GRA-TION

All of Our Books

Available at
amazon

Scan QR code to go to our Instagram for quick access to all of our books or our website
www.labworkspublishing.com